BOSTON

Introduction to Boston

Boston is a fascinating and charming blend of everything old and new in an American metropolis. Her magnificent concrete and glass skyscrapers form pleasing backgrounds to the carefully preserved colonial brick structures. Although modern expressways, broad avenues and elevated transit lines sever the city, narrow twisting streets, red brick sidewalks and gas lights still abound as reminders of a less hurried era.

Boston is not a quaint, compact display that can be quickly seen like a theme amusement park. What makes Boston different and unique is that historical sites and national landmarks are located side-by-side with businesses, hotels, and residential neighborhoods. The people on the streets are by no means all tourists. Shoppers and businessmen share the same sidewalks and restaurants with visitors. Most Bostonians are proud of their city and may usually be depended upon to give directions cheerfully and willingly. It is said that there is still a good deal of the European standard of polite service left in New England's Capital city.

Boston was founded in 1630 and was a cultured metropolis when most of the American Continent was rough frontier. The colorful history of the city includes dealing with Indian Chiefs, hanging witches and fighting hostile armies. The violence remembered in the Boston Tea Party, The Battle of Bunker Hill and the Boston Massacre is contrasted with the serenity of the First Public Park in America (Boston Common) and the Swan Boats in the Public Garden. Boston's glorious past and her attachment to the sea are still preserved along the waterfront where a monument to the builder of the Clipper Ships that made Boston one of the most important ports in the world overlooks a modern jetport across the harbor.

Boston, of course, depended upon the rivers and the sea for its life and commerce years ago and there is still dependence on the sea, but now it is mainly for beauty and recreation. The Charles River separating Boston from Cambridge is flanked by fine parks and the river itself is usually dotted with sailboats and collegiate rowing shells. Glimpses of parks and water wherever one drives or walks are one of the many benefits enjoyed by Bostonians. Another extra advantage is a friendly, cool ocean breeze in the summer and a warming salt wind that quickly melts the winter's snow.

Boston is a city of varying cultures. The Yankees first governed the city, then the Irish Challenged them. Important cultural elements have been added to the spicy mix by Italian, Greek and French restaurants, Jewish delicatessens, a bustling Chinatown and a sizable Spanish-speaking and Black populations.

Visitors marvel at what seems to be an undisciplined look as her citizens ignore the "don't walk" and "no parking" signs. There is an unplanned look because some streets are curved and confusing. These colonial streets twisted to avoid mud flats, inlets and steep hills. When the hills were levelled to fill the flats the streets remained twisted.

More than any other American city, Boston is said to be the most livable city. The culture of museums and institutions of higher learning… a swinging nite-life… a huge population of young adults… only minutes away from summer watering spots and snow covered ski slopes… exciting sports teams… excellent medical and scientific institutions… an historic past and, most of all, a bright future are why the city is so livable. To know Boston is to love Boston… stay a while, meet her people and you too will find that Boston is not only livable, but lovable as well.

The Freedom Trail

The Freedom Trail is a pleasant 2 ½ mile walk (or ride) that covers 20 of Boston's most historic points of interest and many other important landmarks. It is easy to follow the well marked path of red footprints or red bricks that have permanently embedded into the pavement. The sites themselves are indicated by easy-to-find distinctive signs.

Although you can begin anywhere. Boston Common on one end or (the U.S.S. Constitution at the other end are logical) starting points. We suggest parking free at the U.S.S. Constitution. Then, after visiting the ship and the multi-media background show at the Bunker Hill Pavilion, walk the Freedom Trail Backwards and take a cab back to your car from the other end of the Trail. We also suggest you defer your visit to Bunker Hill Monument until the end of the day... then drive up the Hill as this part of the Freedom Trail is the only part that is free from traffic congestion.

Refer to the map on the back cover for additional directions.

The stroll is a journey back into the history of the United States from the events that led to Paul Revere's ride and the American Revolution to the Abolitionist Movement prior to the Civil War.

While walking the Freedom Trail travellers become aware of the commercial and financial heartbeat of the city... the streets, the parks, the stores, the people... In short the Freedom Trail is colorful old Boston and an alert visitor feels he has not only relived the history of Boston, but he knows and has seen how Boston lives and works today.

At most attractions, Senior Citizens and students (with I.D.) are offered reduced admission prices. Please remember that the churches on the Freedom Trail hold regular services which you will wish to respect.

Boston Common

The oldest public park in America dates from 1634 when it was designated as a "Trayning field" for militia and the "feeding of cattell." Near the frog pond (wading is allowed) four witches, several Quakers, and many criminals and pirates were hung in Boston's early years. There's an historic burying ground on the Boylston Street side. Brewer Fountain, designed for the Paris Exhibition of 1855, is near the corner of Park and Tremont Streets. Among the most interesting of many monuments on the Common is the one dedicated to Robert Gould Shaw and the black 54th Regiment which he led in the Civil War. It is located directly across the street from the State House.

State House

The "New" State Capitol building with its dome covered with pure gold dates from 1795. It was designed by Charles Bulfinch, architect of the Nation's Capitol at Washington. In the House Chamber hangs the Sacred Cod (hand carved pine, 58 inches long) emblem of the state's early livelihood. In the Archives Museum are Indian Treaties, the Charter of the Massachusetts Bay Company of 1628 and the oldest written constitution still in effect, The Constitution of 1780. The Hall of Flags displays original battle flags carried by Massachusetts fighting men in 6 wars.

FREE Open Monday to Friday 10 to 4. Closed Holidays and weekends, Guided tours conducted 10 to 3:30.

Park Street Church

At the corner of Park and Tremont Streets is Park Street Church whose steeple was designed by architect Peter Banner and built in 1809. Bostonians still call this the "Brimstone Corner," not because of the fiery sermons, but because gunpowder was stored in the cellar during the war of 1812. Here abolitionist leader William Lloyd Garrison first preached against slavery in 1829 and on July 4th 1831 "America" (My Country'Tis of Thee) was first sung.

Open 9:30 to 3:30 daily. Open Saturday 8:30 to 2:30. Closed Sunday & Monday.

The small structure in the foreground of the picture is the entrance to America's first Subway.

Granary Burying Ground

Next to the Park Street Church on the site of the 'Boston Towne Granary' is the Old Granary Burying Ground. In this famous old cemetery lie 3 signers of the Declaration of Independence; John Hancock, Robert Treat Paine and Samuel Adams; three governors, a chief justice and the victims of the Boston Massacre. A stone inscribed "Mary Goose" is reputed to be the Grave of Mother Goose. The monument in the center marks the grave of Benjamin Franklin's parents.

Open daylight hours.

Statue of Benjamin Franklin

In front of old City Hall on School Street is a statue of Benjamin Franklin. Bronze tablets depict scenes in the life of this famous Bostonian, who was a signer of the Declaration of Independence, a gifted writer, inventor, experimenter with lightning and signer of a treaty with France. As a boy Franklin ran away from his home in Boston to win fame and fortune in Philadelphia.

Site of First Public School

A most unusual plaque has been embedded into the pavement along side the brick path of the Freedom Trail. It marks the site of America's first public school.

In 1635 a school house was built when the town voted that "Philemon Portmort shall be intreated to become schoolmaster for the teaching and nurturing of children." The School, Boston Public Latin school, became the first public school. This was a radical idea in those times as European schooling was generally reserved for the rich, but colonial Bostonians were determined to educate all children.

King's Chapel Burying Ground

Beside King's Chapel on Tremont Street is Boston's oldest cemetery, formerly the vegetable garden of Sir Isaac Johnson whose death-bed wish was that he be buried in his corn and pumpkin patch. Since he was well liked, his friends were buried beside him and for the next 30 years this was Boston's only burying ground.

Here lie William Dawes, Jr. who rode an alternate route in conjunction with Paul Revere to warn of the British advance; John Winthrop, the first Royal Governor of the Massachusetts Bay Colony; and Mary Chilton, first woman to step ashore on Plymouth Rock.

The obelisk (shown in the picture to the left of the Chapel) honors the Chevalier de Saint Sauvier, a French Nobleman who was killed in a street riot by intolerant Bostonians in 1778.

King's Chapel

Organized in 1686 as the first Church of England in Boston, the Church became the First Unitarian Church in America after the Revolution. The present building, complete in 1754, has a bell in the tower cast by Paul Revere.

Open 10:00 to 4:00 daily Closed Holidays and Summer

Old Corner Book Store

Since 1712 this fine example of colonial architecture has housed book-sellers or publishers. Customers of the Bookstore like Longfellow, Emerson, Hawthorne, Holmes, Harriet Beecher Stowe, Whittier and Julia Ward Howe helped make Boston "The Athens of America".

Old South Meeting House

The Old South Meeting House was a Congregational Church built in 1729. As it was the largest hall in Boston, it was also used for some town meetings. One spirited meeting adjourned to become the Boston Tea Party. It is now a museum with exhibits about its role in the Revolution and Colonial Boston.

Open daily 9:30-5 April-Oct. Daily 10-4 Nov. thru March Admission $3.00 Children 6-18 $ 1.00 Senior Citizens & Students $ 2.50.

Site of Benjamin Franklin's Birthplace

At 17 Milk Street around the corner from the Old South Meeting House is a plaque marking the site of the house in which Franklin was born. A bust of Franklin is on the outside of the second story of the building.

The Old State House

Completed in 1713, this building was the Seat of the King's Colonial Government. The State Government moved in when independence from England was an accomplished fact.

The building now houses interesting displays of the history of Boston from its settlement in 1630 to the Great Fire of 1872 which destroyed 776 buildings. Interesting old Boston Police and Fire Department memorabilia are shown. Exhibits of John Hancock's personal possessions, weapons used at the Battle of Bunker Hill, and marine exhibits from Boston's days of glory as world capital for the building of Clipper Ships are worth your time. Admission includes two 9-minute audiovisual presentations "Boston & Paul Revere" and "The growth of Boston."

Admission $ 3.00. School Children; $ 1.00, Boston Seniors and Mass. School children Free; Students and Seniors $ 2.00. Open every day 9:30 - 5 P.M.

Site of the Boston Massacre

A ring of cobblestones in front of the Old State House marks the Revolution's first mass bloodshed. On March 5, 1770 a detachment of nine British troops were so tormented by rock throwing demonstrators that they fired into the crowd. Among the five colonists killed was Crispus Attucks, the first black to die for American Freedom. 11 days earlier a customs official shot a Boston boy, Christopher Snider, who was the first to die in the Revolution.

7

Faneuil Hall

The second President, John Adams, called Faneuil Hall "the cradle of Liberty" because of the lively debates on the new ideas that lead to the Revolutionary War. The building was erected in 1742 as a combination Town Hall and public produce market by Peter Faneuil, a wealthy Boston Merchant. The original old grasshopper weather vane made by Shem Drowne, a colonial craftsman, has pointed the wind direction since 1742. The first floor of the building is occupied by shops and stores in compliance with Faneuil's request. The second floor is an auditorium where meetings of public interest are still frequently held. The third floor is the home and Museum of the Ancient and Honorable Artillery Company, an active military organization since 1638.

> • Hall open 9 to 6 daily. Free Fri. and Sat. 9-7.

The statue in front of Faneuil Hall in Dock Square is Samuel Adams, Governor, patriot and one of the leaders of the events that led to American independence. It's better than an even chance there'll be a pigeon resting on the statue's head.

Faneuil Hall Marketplace and Marketplace Center

In 1826 Mayor Josiah Quincy opened a city-owned marketplace in order to have a central location for the wholesale food industry. In recent years the wholesalers have relocated and the restored Marketplace has become and intriguing world of food, fashion and fun. The Three Building Marketplace has kept its old warmth and charm in the original brick and wood. But contemporary touches to blend yesterday's world with today's have been added in the form of shops and stores full of beautiful and interesting things.

In the center building called the Quincy Market both tourists and residents can sample foods of almost every description – from local seafood specialties to gourmet European Specialties and Oriental delights… And that's only the beginning! Tempting desserts and colorful fresh fruit along with a dramatic array of locally produced artifacts and imported hand-crafted merchandise are on display.

The south Market Building of Faneuil Hall Marketplace features fashions and specialty shops while the North Market Building is devoted to sports, outdoor activities and the world of children. Marketplace Center, next to Quincy Market has interesting pushcarts and shops..SUGGESTION: Plan to eat lunch at Quincy Market, a smorgasbord of take-out food from delicatessen to oriental specialties, pizza, local sea food, cheese, fresh fruit, desserts of every description and much more! It's crowded, and noisy but friendly and great fun!

> • *Marketplace stores and shops Open Monday thru Saturday 10 A.M. to 9 P.M. Sunday Noon to 6 P.M. Restaurants open 7 days a week 'til 2 A.M*

SUGGESTION: Plan to eat lunch at Quincy Market, a smorgasbord of take-out food from delicatessen to oriental specialties, pizza, local sea food, cheese, fresh fruit, desserts of every description and much more! It's crowded, and noisy but friendly and great fun!

The Hancock House and the Boston Stone

...Of special interest... On the way to the Paul Revere House the Freedom Trail leads through narrow, old Marshall Street past the Boston Stone and the Hancock House in Creek Square. The Hancock House is the oldest brick building in Boston. It was first owned by Town Crier William Courser in 1660 and 100 years later by John Hancock.

Across the tiny square is the Boston Stone which was used around 1700 to grind paint pigments by rolling it in a trough. Later the stone and trough were made a part of the outside wall of the building and used as the central measuring point from which distances to Boston were measured.

Haymarket

The visitor walking the Freedom Trail on Friday afternoon or Saturday must pass the 'Haymarket' a delightful but congested old-world-flavored conglomeration of pushcarts selling produce of every kind. The prices are far below supermarket prices and the quality is as good. (Suggestion: buy some fruit to munch as you walk the rest of the trail.)

Union Oyster House

As you walk on Union Street, between Faneuil Hall and The Paul Revere House, you'll pass the Union Oyster House. The original building is about 325 years old. It became a seafood restaurant in 1826 and has been a favorite eating place for prominent Bostonians for more than 150 years. Not only is Union Oyster House the oldest restaurant in Boston, but it is the very oldest restaurant in continuous service in the United States.

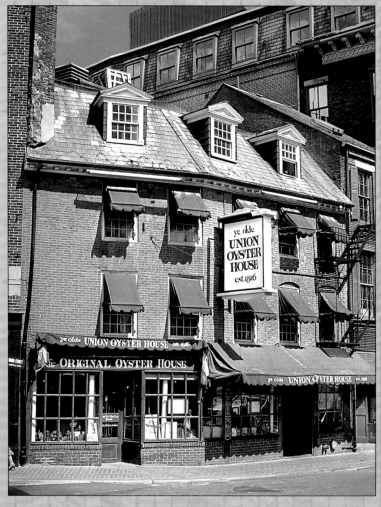

Open 11 A.M. to 9: 30 P.M.,
Fri. & Sat. until 10 P.M.

Paul Revere House

Built around 1676, Paul Revere's House is the oldest house in Boston. It was almost 100 years old when he bought it. Revere and his 16 children (by 2 wives) lived here from 1770 to 1800. The house is authentically furnished as it might have appeared when he left to take part in the Boston Tea Party in 1773 and his famous ride in April of 1775. See Page 20 for a map of Revere's ride.

A NOTE ON PAUL REVERE: Revere was more than a patriot and a night-rider… he was truly one of the country's leading craftsmen and one of the first industrialists and manufacturers. At 22 he was already a master silversmith… considered one of the best of the period. More than

500 magnificent, authentic Revere silver pieces have been preserved and are still widely copied and admired.
During the depression prior to the War for Independence, few Bostonians could afford silver, so Revere became a skilled dentist. After the war he cast cannon for the Continental Army and 400 bells for New England churches. Many of his bells are still in service. He later made and installed the copper and brasswork on Old Ironsides and other Navy ships.
Today the company he founded in 1801 is one of the world leaders in non-ferrous metals… and his spirit still rides in Boston on the Holiday called Patriot's Day every April 19th.
The historic Pierce-Hitchborn House is next door to the Revere House. If you like old homes, there's a combination ticket available.

Open daily 9:30 - 5:15 in summer, 9:30 - 4:15 in winter.
Admission: Adults $ 2.50, Children 5-17 $ 1.00;
Senior and College Students $ 2.00.

PAUL·REVERE

Paul Revere Mall

The famous equestrian statue of Paul Revere by Cyrus Dallin is the focal point of a park in front of The Old North Church.13 bronze tablets set in the brick wall surrounding the park describe the role of area residents in the history of Boston.

St Stephen's Church

Across Hanover Street, opposite the Statue of Paul Revere, is the only remaining church designed by famous Boston architect, Charles Bulfinch. The church was built in 1804.

Old North Church

This gracious, old colonial church dating from 1723 was the highest point on the skyline of Boston when, on the night of April 18, 1775 two lanterns were hung in the steeple. By this signal, Paul Revere who was waiting across the Charles River in Charlestown, learned that the Redcoats were advancing ("...two if by sea...") on Lexington and Concord.

The Old North Church contains the beautifully simple church artifacts of the period and many explanatory plaques. There were some 1100 people buried in the crypts of the church before 1840. The most famous person buried here is Major John Pitcairn, a British Commander killed at Bunker Hill. Church records show that among those buried here are strangers, Indians, and "a Chinese sailor far from home."

Open 9-5 daily Sunday Services 9:00 A.M., 11 A.M. & 4 P.M.

One block up the hill from the Old North Church is Copp's Hill Burying Ground. The site, on high ground overlooking the harbor and entrance to the Charles River, was a strategic point facing Bunker Hill across the water. Here British artillery was trained on the hastily built fortifications on the hills of Charlestown.

The Narrowest House in Boston

Across the street from the Hull Street entrance to Copp's Hill Burying Ground is a house only nine feet six inches Wide. known as Spite House, was said to have been built about 1870 by a man who wanted to shut off light from the home of a neighbor with whom he had quarreled.

Bunker Hill Monument

An impressive granite monument, 221 feet high, marks the location of the Battle of Bunker Hill fought on a hot June 17th in 1775.

Here 1500 Colonial Militia men, under the command of Colonel William Prescott, fortified the hill and held it under sustained attack by 3,000 of General Howe's British regulars during two assaults. While the redcoats marched up the hill in

perfect formation the Americans were told by the commander "Don't fire 'til you see the whites of their eyes!" When the men in homespun opened fire, they felled almost half of the attacking force. The Colonials, out of ammunition, were forced to retreat on the third assault but they won a moral victory and showed that untrained American militia could stand up to the British Regular Army which suffered more than 1,000 casualties that afternoon.

In the course of the battle, much of the town of Charlestown, tinder dry in the hot weather, was destroyed by fires started by the cannon across the river on Copp's Hill.

Energetic visitors who climb the 294 steps to the top of the monument are rewarded with a fine view of Boston Harbor..

Open 9-4:30 daily. FREE Since this is a part of the Boston National Historical Park, Uniformed Park Service people give frequent interpretive talks.

U.S.S. Constitution "Old Ironsides"

Nicknamed "Old Ironsides" when cannon balls bounced off her tough oak planking, this 44-gun frigate is still an officially commissioned U.S. Navy ship. The Constitution is the most famous vessel in the history of the United States Navy. The ship, built by Bostonians like Paul Revere (who furnished the copper and brasswork), was launched in 1797. She sailed through 40 battles and never lost one. Old Ironsides fought pirates m 1803 and 1804 and won a major victory over H.M.S. Guerriere in the War of 1812.

The Constitution is now a living museum of naval history... the sick bay and rum barrels the crew's quarters and the Captain's Cabin, the cannon and the hammocks are just where they were when the frigate was on the high seas.

U.S. Navy personnel are on hand to answer your questions and welcome you aboard.

Open every day 9:30 to 6:00 P.M. Free. Ample free parking. If time is short, plan to come back tomorrow, but don't miss this great ship.

U.S.S. Constitution Museum

Next to the oldest commissioned ship in the world is the U.S.S. Constitution Museum. Here, you can experience for yourself what life was like onboard "Old Ironsides" during her victorious career at sea. Climb an authentic fighting top, swing in a sailor's sleeping hammock, or make the command decisions of a captain making a 1803 ocean crossing through a computer simulation game! Exhibits on the great frigate's construction, her captains life at sea and preservation complete the ship's story. You might even find a model maker at his bench making miniature ships!

Open 9 - 5 daily. Adults $4.00; Senior & Students $3.00; Children $2.00. Children under 5 free.

The Bunker Hill Pavilion...

Only a few yards from the USS Constitution is the Bunker Hill Pavilion with its multi-media recreation of The Battle of Bunker Hill. In the specially built amphi-theatre the visitor is surrounded by the sights and sounds of the battle. Seven sound channels and 14 projection screens are employed to surround the audience with a sense of realism. A most impressive presentation... Interesting and entertaining for the whole family.

Adults $3.00; Children $1.50 Family rate is $8.00 family unit. Open daily 9: 30 A.M. - 4:30 P.M. April-Nov.

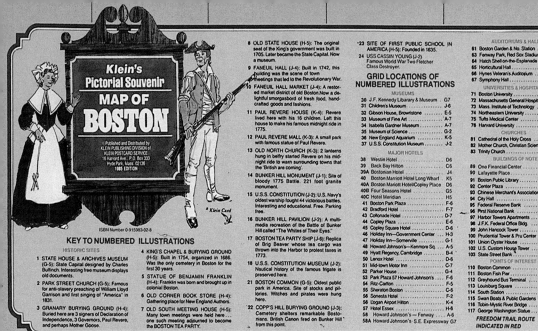

Klein's Pictorial Souvenir MAP OF BOSTON

Published and Distributed by
KLEIN PUBLISHING DIVISION of
KLEIN POSTCARD SERVICE
16 Harvard Ave. • P.O. Box 333
Hyde Park, Mass. 02136
1985 EDITION

ISBN Number 0-915983-02-8

"Klein Card"

KEY TO NUMBERED ILLUSTRATIONS

HISTORIC SITES

1 STATE HOUSE & ARCHIVES MUSEUM (G-5): State Capital designed by Charles Bulfinch. Interesting free museum displays old documents.

2 PARK STREET CHURCH (G-5): Famous for anti-slavery preaching of William Lloyd Garrison and first singing of "America" in 1831.

3 GRANARY BURYING GROUND (H-4): Buried here are 3 signers of Declaration of Independence, 3 Governors, Paul Revere, and perhaps Mother Goose.

4 KING'S CHAPEL & BURYING GROUND (H-5): Built in 1754, organized in 1686. Was the only cemetery in Boston for the first 30 years.

5 STATUE OF BENJAMIN FRANKLIN (H-4): Franklin was born and brought up in colonial Boston.

6 OLD CORNER BOOK STORE (H-4): Gathering place for New England Authors.

7 OLD SOUTH MEETING HOUSE (H-5): Many town meetings were held here ... one such meeting adjourned to become the BOSTON TEA PARTY.

8 OLD STATE HOUSE (H-5): The original seat of the King's government was built in 1705. Later became the State Capital. Now a museum.

9 FANEUIL HALL (J-4): Built in 1742, this building was the scene of town meetings that led to the Revolutionary War.

10 FANEUIL HALL MARKET (J-4): A restored market district of old Boston.Now a delightful smorgasbord of fresh food, hand-crafted goods and fashions.

11 PAUL REVERE HOUSE (K-4): Revere lived here with his 16 children. Left this house to make his famous midnight ride in 1775.

12 PAUL REVERE MALL (K-3): A small park with famous statue of Paul Revere.

13 OLD NORTH CHURCH (K-3): 2 lanterns hung in belfry started Revere on his midnight ride to warn surrounding towns that the "British are coming!"

14 BUNKER HILL MONUMENT (J-1): Site of bloody 1775 Battle. 221 foot granite monument.

15 U.S.S. CONSTITUTION (J-2): U.S. Navy's oldest warship fought 44 victorious battles. Interesting and educational. Free. Parking free.

16 BUNKER HILL PAVILION (J-2): A multi-media recreation of the Battle of Bunker Hill called "The Whites of Their Eyes."

17 BOSTON TEA PARTY SHIP (J-6): Replica of Brig Beaver whose tea cargo was thrown into the Harbor to protest taxes in 1773.

18 U.S.S. CONSTITUTION MUSEUM (J-2): Nautical history of the famous frigate is preserved here.

21 BOSTON COMMON (G-5): Oldest public park in America. Site of stocks and pillories. Witches and pirates were hung here.

*22 COPP'S HILL BURYING GROUND (J-3): Cemetery shelters remarkable Bostonians. British Canon fired on Bunker Hill from this point.

*23 SITE OF FIRST PUBLIC SCHOOL IN AMERICA (H-5): Founded in 1635.

24 USS CASSIN YOUNG (J-2): Famous World War Two Fletcher Class Destroyer.

GRID LOCATIONS OF NUMBERED ILLUSTRATIONS

MUSEUMS

30 J.F. Kennedy Library & Museum	G7
31 Children's Museum	J-6
32 Gibson House, Brownstone	E-5
33 Museum of Fine Art	A-7
34 Isabella Gardner Museum	A-7
35 Museum of Science	E-3
36 New England Aquarium	K-5
37 U.S.S. Constitution Museum	J-2

MAJOR HOTELS

38 Westin Hotel	D6
39 Back Bay Hilton	C6
39A Bostonian Hotel	J4
40 Boston Marriott Hotel Long Wharf	K5
40A Boston Marriott Hotel/Copley Place	D6
40B Four Seasons Hotel	G5
40C Hotel Meridian	H5
41 Boston Park Plaza	F-6
42 Bradford Hotel	F-7
43 Colonade Hotel	D-7
44 Copley Plaza	E-6
45 Copley Square Hotel	D-6
49 Holiday Inn—Government Center	H-3
47 Holiday Inn—Somerville	G-1
48 Howard Johnson's—Kenmore Sq.	A-5
49 Hyatt Regency, Cambridge	B-4
50 Lenox Hotel	D-6
51 Mid-town Motor Inn	C-7
52 Parker House	G-4
53 Park Plaza 57 Howard Johnson's	F-6
54 Ritz-Carlton	F-5
55 Sheraton Boston	C-6
56 Sonesta Hotel	F-2
56 Logan Airport Hilton	K-4
57 Hotel Essex	H-6
58 Howard Johnson's — Fenway	A-6
58A Howard Johnson's S.E. Expressway	G7

AUDITORIUMS & HALLS

61 Boston Garden & No. Station	H-3
63 Fenway Park, Red Sox Stadium	A-6
64 Hatch Shell on-the-Esplanade	E-4
65 Horticultural Hall	C-7
66 Hynes Veteran's Auditorium	C-7
67 Symphony Hall	C-7

UNIVERSITIES & HOSPITALS

71 Boston University	A-4
72 Massachusetts General Hospital	G-2
73 Mass. Institute of Technology	B-4
74 Northeastern University	B-7
75 Tufts Medical Center	G-6
76 Harvard University	A-4

CHURCHES

81 Cathedral of the Holy Cross	E-7
82 Mother Church, Christian Science	C-7
83 Trinity Church	E-6

BUILDINGS OF NOTE

89 One Financial Center	H-2
90 Lafayette Place	G-5
91 Boston Public Library	G-5
92 Center Plaza	H-4
93 Chinese Merchant's Association	G-6
94 City Hall	H-4
95 Federal Reserve Bank	H-6
96 Frst National Bank	H-5
97 Harbor Towers Apartments	K-5
98 J.F.K. Federal Office Bldg.	H-4
99 John Hancock Tower	E-6
100 Prudential Tower & Pru Center	D-6
101 Union Oyster House	J-4
102 U.S. Custom House Tower	J-5
103 State Street Bank	J-5

POINTS OF INTEREST

110 Boston Common	G-5
111 Boston Fish Pier	L-7
112 Greyhound Bus Terminal	F-6
113 Louisburg Square	G-4
114 South Station	H-6
115 Swan Boats & Public Gardens	F-5
116 Tobin-Mystic River Bridge	K-1
117 George Washington Statue	F-5

**FREEDOM TRAIL ROUTE
INDICATED IN RED**

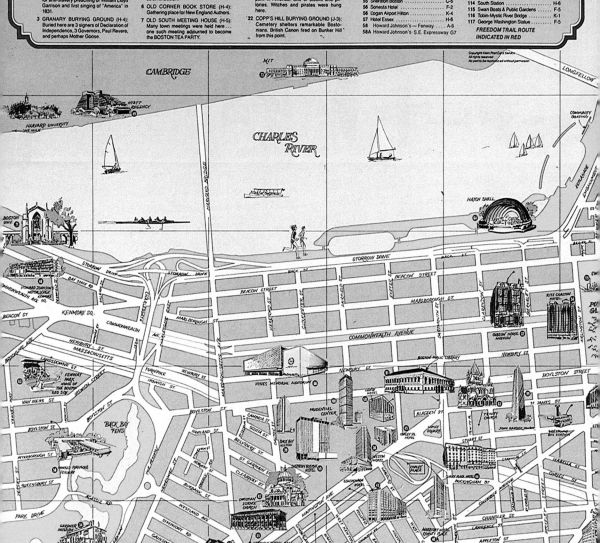

A Bird's Eye View of Boston

The Mother Church of Christian Science and its reflecting pool are seen in the foreground. The Hilton and Sheraton Hotels and the Prudential Center are at the left. The Colonnade, Westin and Marriott Hotels and Copley Place shopping mall are in front of the dark mirrored surface of the Hancock Tower. Downtown and Boston Harbor are in the background. The sailboat-dotted Charles River is seen at the left.

The Boston Tea Party Ship and Museum

On a raw December night in 1773 angry Bostonians, some disguised as Indians, boarded 3 British ships, The Beaver, The Dartmouth, and the Eleanor and dumped 342 chests of East India Tea weighing 90,000 pounds into the harbor.

This violence was in protest of a tax of 3 pence a pound which the citizens of Boston, who had no voice in making the laws or levying the taxes, felt was taxation without representation.

The event, known in history as the Boston Tea Party, look place only after repeated appeals to the local authorities for relief, and mass meetings and other demonstrations proved useless.

The actual boarding and work was done by 40 to 50 costumed and disguised men and several hundred others who were attending a town meeting

The Boston Waterfront

on the tax at the Old South Meeting House. The men were disciplined and quiet. They did no harm to the rest of the cargo or the vessels themselves.

As a result of the Tea Party, the British Government closed the port of Boston forcing upon the colonists additional hardships which led to the War for Independence.

The authentic replica of the Beaver and the Tea Party Museum are on permanent exhibition at the Congress Street Bridge on Boston's waterfront.

John Hancock Tower

Located in the heart of Copley Square in Boston's Back Bay Area, this magnificent building was design by E.M. Pei.

This 52 story building, is New England's tallest structure and is an important part of Boston's identity and image.

The Midnight Ride Of Paul Revere

On the night of April 18, 1775, Paul Revere crossed Boston Harbor and rode to warn the towns west of Boston that British troops were marching to seize arms stored in Lexington and Concord. As a result of this warning, the first clashes of arms in the War for Independence occurred at Lexington Green and Concord Bridge.

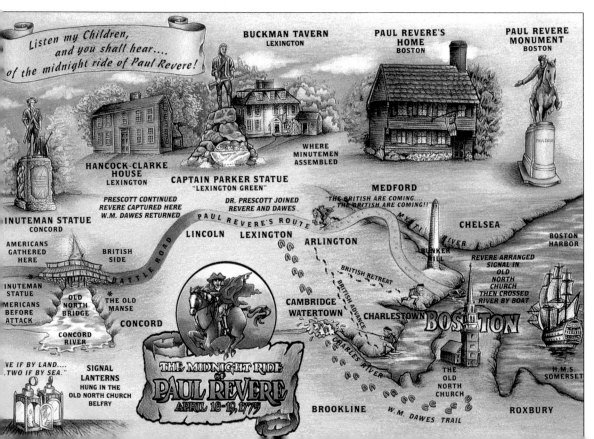

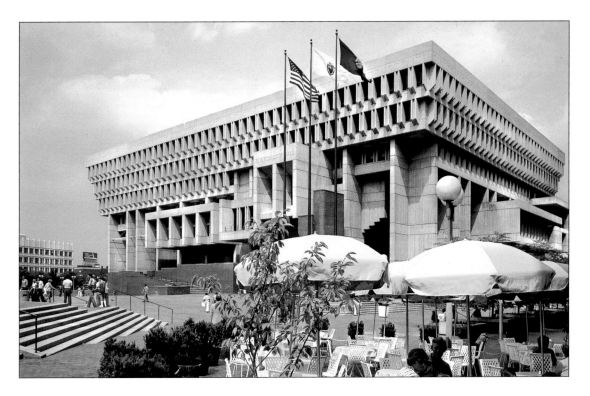

City Hall and Government Center

Boston's imaginative City Hall is dramatically accentuated by a sunken fountain and broad brick plazas. This award winning public building is adjacent to the twin-towered John F. Kennedy Federal Building, The Leverett Saltonstall State office building, and the curving skyscraper laying on its side called Center Plaza. The area is collectively called Government Center… and it is, perhaps, the city's most dramatic change in appearance in this century.

What is now Government Center was, up until the 1950's, Scollay Square… noted for its burlesque houses, drinking places, and other places of unsavory reputation. If Grandpa or Uncle Charlie is looking for an area in which he had some wild times during World War II, tell him it's been completely changed.

Boston National Historical Park

Several important historic sites in Boston have been grouped together as a National Historical Park. These locations are administered by their traditional owners with the help of the National Park Service.

Permanent, informative bronze markers have been placed at these sites by National Park Service and federally trained personnel give frequent interpretive talks and are often available to answer your questions at these locations.

The National Park sites are The Old State house, Old North Church, Faneuil Hall, The Old South Meeting House, Paul Revere's House, Bunker Hill, the Navy Yard where the U.S.S. Constitution and the U.S.S. Cassin Young (a WW II destroyer) may be seen, and Dorchester Heights.

Dorchester Heights (10 minutes South of Downtown in South Boston) were fortified in a single night's work using cannon laboriously hauled from Fort Ticonderoga. This show of strength forced the British to evacuate Boston in 1776.

This guide book uses the arrowhead symbol to designate Boston National Park Sites. A visitors' center where rest room facilities, information and a free audio-visual program are available is maintained by the National Park Service at 15 State Street (across from the entrance to the Old State House). The Visitors Center has facilities for the handicapped. You may phone them at (617) 242-5642.

Boston is a modern city-on-the-move. The brownstones and the low-rise marble mansions in the rest of the Back Bay are protected from high-rise development by Law as an Architectural Historic District. The new skyscrapers have enhanced the open spaces with reflective pools and plazas. They have done much to keep the City livable by providing needed facilities like the John B. Hynes Auditorium and Convention Center, modern department stores, hotels and specialty shops.

Lady visitors will love the smaller shops and galleries on Newbury Street where a shopping spree may be costly as the area caters to the carriage trade. Children (and tired mothers) will love an inexpensive and relaxing ride on the swan boats in the Public Garden (bring bread for the ducks

Boston' Back Bay

It is difficult for even native Bostonians to understand that the most beautiful part of their city was nothing but tidal mud flats before 1860. It was actually the Back Bay of the Charles River. The district includes the entire Public Garden where the Swan Boats now glide, Copley Square with its beautifully landscaped park area, Trinity and the Old South Churches, The Hancock Tower (New England's tallest building), the entire Prudential Center, Kenmore Square, the residential areas along one of the Nation's most beautiful streets – Commonwealth Avenue, famed Beacon Street, and more!

Back Bay is beautiful because while it was being filled and developed the middle and working class people could more easily afford and preferred East Boston or South Boston. As a result impressive atone and brick mansions designed by the period's best architects were built. These fine homes were ornately furnished with costly hand-carved woodwork and imported works of art by the people who made Boston the leading cultural city in the hemisphere.

On any street map or from the observation decks at the Top of the Prudential or Hancock towers it is easy to see that the broad Back Bay streets were well planned in orderly rows.

They were even named alphabetically. Starting at the edge of the Public Garden we have Arlington, Berkeley, Clarendon, Dartmouth, Exeter, Fairfield and Hereford Street. This neat area sharply contrasts with the twisting streets of the older part of the city along the Freedom Trail.

The most impressive feature of the Back Bay is its backbone of new skyscrapers. The Hancock Tower, The Prudential Center and the Christian Science Church Complex give the impression that

and peanuts for the squirrels). History buffs and art lovers will admire the fine statuary and the inscriptions on Boylston and Arlington Streets along the edge of the Public Garden. A plaque near the corner of Charles and Beacon Streets marks the spot where the British boarded boats to cross the river on the way to Concord and Lexington in 1775 (remember?… two if by sea). Yet the spot is more than a quarter mile from the Charles over filled-in land.

Gourmets will enjoy the fine selection of French, Hungarian or seafood specialty restaurants in the Back Bay which is also famous for its moderately priced steak houses, Italian restaurants and sandwich shops. After dinner we suggest a visit to Boston's liveliest nite clubs in and near Kenmore Square.

The Back Bay declined when the automobile gave the wealthy residents access to the city from outlying suburbs, but the fine buildings and gracious open spaces remained and the spirit of the soaring new high-rise buildings has brought a renewed bright future to Boston's Back Bay.

SUGGESTION: There's a well-preserved, Back Bay Victorian, brownstone townhouse filled with 19th century furniture on permanent display at 137 Beacon Street. From June thru October you can visit it Wed. - Sun. (except Holidays). From November thru May open Saturday & Sunday. GIBSON HOUSE is open 1-3 p.m. Guided tours. Admission $5.00. Phone: 267-6338.

Dining Out in Boston

Bostonians feel that one can get a better meal by accident in Boston than he can on purpose in most other parts of the country. Of course, this does not apply to your home town.

There are a multitude of very good restaurants all around the city and you'll find the fast food franchises in numerous locations.

Many eating places make Boston's unsurpassed seafood the specialty of the house. There are steakhouses galore and, if your taste runs to foreign style, there are French, Greek and Italian restaurants.

Boston's chinatown features Cantonese style cooking... it's delicious and relatively inexpensive. The city has Hungarian restaurants, Kosher delicatessens, Japanese, Indian, German and Arabic places to eat as well as ice cream shops of every description. If you can't find what food you're looking for in Boston, it doesn't exist!

Rather than prepare an incomplete list of restaurants, we suggest you see the yellow pages of your phone book .

...And would you believe you can visit hundreds of restaurants in Boston without finding Boston Baked Beans on the menu...?

But almost every Boston restaurant features Clam Chowder, New England or Boston style. Make it at home using the recipe below.

BOSTON BAKED BEANS - Traditional recipe

Baked at 300 degrees for 3-1/2 hours. Servers 8

1	package (1 pound) navy or pea beans.
1/4	pound salt pork, cut in 2 pieces
1	teaspoon dry mustard
6	cups water
1/3	cup molasses
1	teaspoon salt
1/2	teaspoon baking soda
3	tablespoon sugar
1/4	teaspoon pepper
1	small whole onion peeled

1. Soak beans overnight in a large sauce pan in 6 cups of water. Add baking soda. Heat to boiling and simmer 10 minutes. Drain in colander over a large bowl. Save liquid.
2. Place beans, salt pork and onion in a bean pot or casserole. Add molasses, salt, sugar, dry mustard, pepper and a cup of liquid. Stir thoroughly. Add enough liquid to cover the beans. Cover bean pot or casserole.
3. Bake 2 hours at 300 degrees. Add the rest of the liquid and stir again. Bake an additional 1-1/2 hours (or until beans ar tender.) Uncover last 1/2 hour.

Cheers from Boston

On the corner of Beacon and Charles Streets, across from Boston Common, is the pub made famous by the T.V. Series "Cheers". They'll happily serve your favorite beverage and supply you with souvenirs of your good time in Boston. You might also enjoy a tour of the city in a horse drawn victorian carriage

Beacon Hill

The beacon on Boston's highest hill warning residents of danger from attacking Indians or hostile armies has long since disappeared. Indeed, the top 60 feet of the hill itself was cut off and used to fill in the mud flats of the Charles River. But the hill, crowned with the 'new' State House (built in 1795 by Charles Bulfinch, architect of the Capitol at Washington) is still an important part of the city.

Most visitors see the front side of the hill facing Boston Common, but it is the back slope of the hill facing the Charles River that deserves more attention. The Nation's oldest residential area has brick sidewalks, gas lights, bootscrapers by interesting doorways and many cobblestone streets. Here wealthy Bostonians have their townhouses within easy walking distant of downtown financial districts, and young artists and students share apartments handy to Boston's night-life and Universities. Acorn Street (off West Cedar and Willow) is paved with river stones. Off Pinkney Street is Louisburg Square, a delightful private park surrounded by townhouses of Boston's oldest families.

Charles Street, the main street of this quaint neighborhood, is usually bright with flowers and colorful umbrellas of sidewalk restaurants… and much of the street is lined with antique shops, boutiques, bookstores and specialty shops for browsers and seekers of unusual gifts. The area is a Registered National Historic Landmark and is a living reminder of how Boston looked in the 1850's.

RECIPE FOR NEW ENGLAND CLAM CHOWDER

2	6 1/2 oz, cans or 8 oz. frozen or 2 cups minced fresh clams with all their liquid
2	medium potatoes, diced
1	generous pinch pepper
1	medium onion, diced
5	strips bacon
1 1/2	cups water
1/4	cup flour
1	teaspoon salt
*3	cups milk

1. Cook bacon in 3 or 4 quart pot until crisp. Remove and drain Bacon. Pour off all but 2 tablespoons grease. Add onion and saute until translucent.
2. Add potatoes, water, clams, salt, pepper and shake in flour. Stir. Cover pot and simmer 12 minutes or until potatoes are tender.
3. Add milk. Crumble in bacon. Heat, stirring occasionally until hot, without boiling.

YIELDS 2 QUARTS

* For richer chowder use light cream or 1/2 & 1/2 and top with a pat of butter.

The Museums of Boston

Boston ranks high among the cities of the world in displays of scientific and artistic achievement as well as the history that shaped our country and the wonders of the world of nature. In addition to the fine historic displays at points of interest along the Freedom Trail, there are as many other noteworthy exhibits as one has time to visit. Here are the facts on these museum in capsule form. Prices and hours are, of course, subject to change. Some are free to young children... And senior citizens and students usually rate a discount. Holiday hours vary, we suggest you phone if you plan a visit on a Holiday.

The Presidential museum at the John F. Kennedy Library

New England Aquarium	*An exciting, new building on the waterfront features a 200,000 gallon glass tank in which thousands of exotic fish are exhibited in life-like environment. Much to see. Don't miss performing dolphin or sea lion shows.*
Museum of Science	*Lively atmosphere, colorful do-it-yourself exhibits. Everything in science from pre-historic monsters to space capsules. Special live demonstrations throughout the day. Special dinosaur exhibit.*
Museum of Fine Arts	*Man's visual world from remote antiquity to today. One of the most comprehensive museums the Western Hemisphere. Paintings by masters, sculptures, Greek & Roman art, etc. Frequent special exhibitions.*
The Presidential Museum at the John F. Kennedy Library	*The life and times of the President J.F. Kennedy in a dramatic setting overlooking Boston Harbor. Documents, artifacts, films & slide presentations.*
The Children's Museum	*Fun for children...a learning experience. Staffed by professionals who know what kids like. Children don't just watch, they participate in all of the exhibits.*
Harvard University museums	*4 museums under 1 roof: Zoology, Geology, Botany and Museums Anthropology (Peabody Museum). Displays of natural history and objects from many cultures. Noted for unequalled beauty of glass flowers in the Botanical section.*
Isabella Stewart Gardner museum	*Italian style palace houses art assembled by Isabella Gardner. Noted for paintings, tapestries, stained glass windows and fine period furniture.*
The Arnold Arboretum	*America's Greatest Garden. 265 Acres containing 7000 varieties of trees and shrubs from all over the north temperate zone. Spectacular seasonal displays of lilacs and other flowering shrubs. Free Greenhouse Tours Wed. Afternoons. Outside Bonsai display June-Oct.*

Close to downtown, Freedom Trail & Quincy Market. On Central Wharf. Parking across the street. 973 5200.	9-6 daily Wed.-Thurs. 9-8 Sat., Sun. and Holidays 9-7	Adults $ 11.50 Kind 3-11,$ 5.50 Under 3, Free Elders $ 8.50	Fascinating for the whole family. Cool & relaxing. Half price before 9 AM.
On a bridge between Boston & Cambridge at Science Park. 723-2500. Park at a Nominal Fee.	Daily 9-7 Friday 9-9 PM	Adults $9.00 Kids 3-11, $7.00 Elders $7.00 Under 3, Free	Plenty of interest for everyone. Allow. at least 1/2 day.
Near Northeastern U. Close to Pru Center. 465 Huntington Ave. 267-9300	10-4:45 everyday Wed. until 9:45 Wed. admission by voluntary contribution	Adults $10.00, Kids Under 17 free with adult Elders and Students $8.00	A must for lovers of art and ancient civilizations
On Morrissey Blvd. 5 mins. South of Downtown. Free parking. 929-4523	9-5 daily Closed major Holidays	Adults $8:00 Kids 6-12 Free Elders & Students $6.00	Modern history comes alive. Interesting and educational
Museum Wharf on waterfront 300 Congress St., Boston 426-8855	Tues.-Sun.10-5 Sunday 1-5 PM Freday'til 9 Closed Mon. Sept.- June	Adults $7.00 Kinds 2-15, $6.00 $1.00 Fri.eve 5-9	Little kids love it. Parents learn too.
Near Harvard Square on Harvard Campus. Oxford St. or Divinity Ave., Cambridge 495-9400	Daily 10-5 Sunday 1-5 PM Free on Wednesday	Adults $5.00 Students $3.00 Elders $4.00 Under 18, Free	Of great interest to students, rockhounds, flower lovers & animal enthusiasts
Fenway Court. 10 minutes from Pru Center or Kenmore Square. 566-1401	11-5 daily Closed Monday	Adults $10.00 Seniors $7.00, Students $5.00, 2-17, $3.00	Not for kids Magnificent European art in unique setting.
Jamaica Plain, 10 min. from downtown. 524-1717 for directions & what's in bloom, special events	Dawn to dusk every day	Free. Drive-thru available for elderly & handicapped.	Great for gardeners. Much walking Special tours Special events

The Waterfront

In recent years the warehouse and dock area on Boston's waterfront has been undergoing a transformation to recreational and residential use. What only a few years ago were old piers and freight sheds are now desirable apartments, handsome restaurants, shops and galleries. New high-rise apartments can be seen alongside Boston's fine Aquarium on Atlantic Avenue only a five minute walk from Faneuil Hall.

In the Aquarium area there are several Coast Guard approved tour boats to take you on a cruise around Boston Harbor (fare averages $6, 1/2 price for children). If dad and brother have the time, there are many "party boats" offering a

half-day's deep-sea fishing trip including lines and bait at reasonable prices. There are also several whale-watching boats which will take you to the feeding grounds of huge whales where you'll be awed by their antics.

Cross the Northern Avenue bridge (off Atlantic Avenue) and you will easily find 2 of Boston's most famous seafood restaurant (Pier 4, and Jimmy's). On the Fish pier there is usually plenty to see. Despite a marked decline in the past decade, plenty of fish is still caught by the Boston Fishing Fleet and processed here.

Half-way out on the pier there's a restaurant with no sign outside. The No Name Restaurant at 15 1/2 Fish Pier serves great fish dinners and luncheons at reasonable prices. Ask any one on the pier where it is.

Even if you don't plan to buy anything, visit a live lobster dealer. If you're not a New Englander, you'll learn how lobsters are kept alive in pools of circulating ocean water and how carefully they are packed for shipment. Note the price and you'll understand why the price of your lobster dinner was so high.

You won't be able to see Boston Light unless you take a harbor cruise, but little Brewster Island is the oldest lighthouse location on the continent.

Since 1670 a beacon here has welcomed ships into the harbor. The first lighthouse (built in 1713) was blown up by British Marines during the Revolution. The present lighthouse was built in 1783. In 1719 Boston Light developed the world's first fog-warning signal when a cannon was fired at regular intervals during heavy fog.

Boston's old harbor fortification may be seen at Castle Island Park in South Boston (a 15 minute ride from downtown, free parking). On Castle Island facing the open sea there is a monument to Donald McKay who designed and built the fastest Clipper Ships. McKay's graceful sailing ships brought prosperity to the port of Boston in the 1850's, and set speed records that are still unequalled.

Celtics

Fenway Park

There's always major league sports activity in Boston as professional sports are played here every season. Major sports teams are:

Baseball . . . . Red Sox
Basketball . . . . Celtics
Hockey . . . . Bruins
Football . . . . Patriots
Soccer . . . . Revolution

Racing fans will find dog racing at Wonderland. If you would like to play golf or tennis, there are scores of public golf courses and tennis courts to choose from. The many college varsity teams from local Universities can also provide entertainment for the visitor. Check the newspaper sports for what's happening today.

Gillette Stadium

Bruins

Sports Excitement in Boston

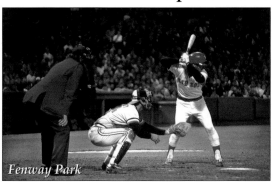
Fenway Park

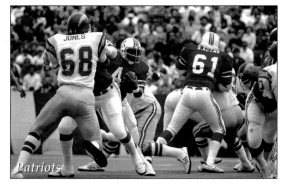
Patriots

Cambridge the University City
HARVARD SQUARE AND HARVARD UNIVERSITY
Harvard Square, crossroads for students from all over the world, has many boutiques and bookshops. The country's oldest institution of higher learning (Harvard) was founded here in 1636. The Square is always crowded with interesting people

HARVARD YARD AND MEMORIAL CHAPEL
There's a delightful, old-style campus hidden behind tall brick walls just off bustling Harvard Square. Here students attending the country's oldest institution of higher learning cross the green lawns of "The Yard" on their way to and from classes.

MASSACHUSETTS INSTITUTE OF TECHNOLOGY

Since its founding in 1861, M.I.T. has become one of the world's foremost technical institutions. The five major departments of the University include Science, Engineering, Humanities, Social Science and Architecture which are taught on a beautiful campus across the Charles River from Boston.

HARVARD UNIVERSITY

The Weeks footbridge joins portions of the campus of Harvard University which is divided by the beautiful Charles River. Harvard, the country's oldest institution of higher learning, was founded in 1636

Lexington...

A few miles west of Boston (take Route 2 and follow signs) is Lexington Green, the scene of the first clash of arms of the American Revolution on April 19, 1775.

Clustered around the Green are many carefully preserved, historic buildings and monuments. The statue of Captain John Parker, in command of the Minutemen, stands guard over the scene. It was Capt. Parker who said, "Dont fire unless fired upon. But if they mean to have a war, let it begin here."

See Harrington House, Buckman Tavern, many battle monuments and the Old Belfrey. Get full information at visitor's center.

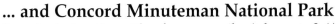

... and Concord Minuteman National Park

From Lexington Green it's a few more miles (take route 2-A) west to Concord, where the British marched after the Battle at Lexington. Stop at Minuteman National Historical Park Visitor's Center on Route 2-A for descriptive literature, free Minuteman Statue at Concord movies and interpretive slide presentations. Then visit the North Bridge in the National Park. It was here that another skirmish took place on the first day of fighting. If time allows, there are many historical homes and museums to see in the vicinity.

Suburban Boston is resplendent with autumn foliage color. If you possibly can do so. visit Concord and Lexington during the first half of October.